GEORGES BIZET.
1838—1875.

CARMEN

Opera in Four Acts

By

GEORGES BIZET

Words by

H. MEILHAC and L. HALEVY

Adapted from the Novel by
PROSPER MÉRIMÉE

English Version by
RUTH AND THOMAS MARTIN

Ed. 421

G. SCHIRMER *New York / London*

NOTE

G. SCHIRMER, INC.

CARMEN.

FIRST PERFORMED AT THE OPÉRA-COMIQUE, PARIS, MARCH 3, 1875.

Characters of the Drama,

With the Original Cast as presented at the first performance.

DON JOSÉ, Corporal of Dragoons	M. Lhérie.
ESCAMILLO, Toreador	M. Bouhy.
ZUNIGA, Captain of Dragoons	M. Dufriche.
MORALES, Officer	M. Duvernoy.
LILLAS PASTIA, Innkeeper	M. Nathan.
CARMEN, a Gypsy-girl	Mme. Galli-Marié.
MICAELA, a Village maiden	Mlle. Chapuy.
FRASQUITA } Companions of Carmen	Mlle. Ducasse.
MERCEDES }	Mlle. Chevalier.
EL DANCAÏRO } Smugglers.	
EL REMENDADO }	
A GUIDE.	

Dragoons, Gypsies, Smugglers, Cigarette-girls, Street-boys, etc.

ACT I.—A PUBLIC SQUARE IN SEVILLA.   ACT II.—LILLAS PASTIA'S TAVERN.
ACT III.—A WILD MOUNTAIN-PASS.   ACT IV.—PUBLIC SQUARE IN
SEVILLA AT THE ENTRANCE OF THE CIRCUS.

The Story of Carmen.

The scene of the opera is Sevilla and environs; the time, 1820.   Act I opens in a square of Sevilla.   *Morales*, officer of dragoons, is lounging, with the soldiers of the guard, in front of the guard-house, watching the people come and go. Among them he notices a maiden, *Micaela,* whose shy glances betray an interest in the soldiers.   Questioning her, he finds that she wishes to see *Don José*, a corporal in the regiment; she then evades too pressing attentions, and leaves the square. The relief-guard, with *Don José* and his captain, *Zuniga,* appears, and the other guard marches off.   Now, at the stroke of noon, the cigarette-girls pour out from the adjacent tobacco-factory; last of all comes *Carmen*, the beautiful, bold, heartless Gypsy-girl.   Scoffing at the gallants who crowd around to seek her favor, her eye chances to light on *Don José*, still quite oblivious of her presence.   He takes her fancy; after momentary hesitation she approaches him, throws him a nosegay, and, with a passionate glance, turns and flees.   *Don José*, amazed and, against his will, flattered by such a token of partiality, is presently surprised by his village sweetheart, *Micaela,* who brings a message from his mother, exhorting him to be true to his first love. *Micaela* discreetly withdraws while *Don José* reads the letter; filled with tender thoughts of earlier days, he would renounce the fitful passion inspired by *Carmen;*—but a sudden disturbance breaks in upon this softer mood; *Carmen* has wounded one of her companions in a quarrel, and *Don José* himself is commissioned by *Zuniga* to arrest her and take her to jail. But her passionate wiles overbear his good resolutions; he lets her escape, and is punished by imprisonment.

Act II plays in a suburban resort of smugglers, of whom *Carmen* is a faithful ally. Here she had promised to meet *Don José;* just now she is passing the time agreeably in the company of *Zuniga* and other officers. *Escamillo,* a redoubtable *toreador,* joins them, and falls in love with *Carmen,* who repulses his advances. Two Gypsies, leaders of the smugglers, enter to inform *Carmen* and her two companions *Frasquita* and *Mercedes,* that their aid is needed, the same evening, to pass some "merchandise". *Carmen,* awaiting *Don José,* who has just been set at liberty, refuses to go. He comes; the rest retire, leaving him alone with *Carmen,* who, enchanted at recovering her lover, employs all her art to entertain and fascinate him. But, of a sudden, he hears distant bugles sounding the "retreat", realizes that he will be treated as a deserter if absent without leave, and, despite *Carmen's* astonishment and growing disdain and fury, is in the act of departing, when the door is forced by *Zuniga.* He peremptorily orders *Don José* to be gone, who as haughtily refuses to yield to his rival; swords are drawn, but *Carmen* summons the Gypsies from their hiding-places. *Zuniga* is disarmed, and *Don José* is forced, as an open mutineer against his superior officer, to leave Sevilla and join the smugglers.

In Act III the band is assembled within a wild mountain-gorge, waiting to carry their bales into the city. *Don José* is also there; but he takes no interest in their enterprise, and bitter regrets continually assail him. *Carmen,* already tired of her half-hearted lover, tauntingly advises him to go back to his mother; she persists in tormenting him, although the cards, in which she implicitly believes, foretell that she is doomed to the speedy death which his gloomy looks presage. The band departs, leaving *Don José* to mount guard over goods left behind for another trip. *Micaela,* unseen by him, approaches; she catches sight of *Don José,* but at the same instant he levels his carbine and fires in her direction. Overcome by fright, she swoons and sinks down behind the rocks. The shot, however, was aimed at *Escamillo,* who clambers unharmed over the rocks, and introduces himself to *Don José,* whose pleasure at their meeting is quickly turned to bitterest hatred when *Escamillo* nonchalantly announces his errand—to meet *his* sweetheart, *Carmen.* A terrible duel ensues, fought with the deadly *navajas* (large, keen-bladed clasp-knives). *Escamillo's* life is saved by the unexpected intervention of *Carmen,* whose love is now wholly transferred to him ; and leaves the scene defiantly. The smugglers are about to follow, when they espy *Micaela,* who, awakened from her swoon, implores *Don José* to hasten to his dying mother. Unable to resist this appeal, he goes but warns *Carmen* that they will meet again elsewhere.

The scene of Act IV is another square in Sevilla, before the ancient amphitheatre in which the bull-fights are held.   Last in the brilliant procession formed by the participants in the combat, comes *Escamillo*, with him *Carmen*, radiant with delight in her latest conquest.   Her friends warn her to go away, telling her that *Don José* is lying in wait.   She does not heed the warning.   The two meet.   *Don José* is in no murderous mood ; for the time, love has wholly gained the mastery.   He implores *Carmen* to be his, even promises to rejoin the band of smugglers for her sake. She repels him with inflexible determination ; laughs him to scorn, and throws at his feet the ring he had given her; fearlessly confronting his rising fury, she tells him that all is over between them, that *Escamillo* is everything to her, and that, though she feels that death is near, she will love him to her last breath.   Exulting in the outburst of applause from the arena, telling of *Escamillo's* triumph, she attempts to join him; but *Don José*, maddened by jealousy, seizes her and stabs her to the heart at the very moment when *Escamillo*, flushed by victory, issues from the amphitheatre with the exultant throng.

The plot here sketched in outline, is based on Prosper Mérimée's story, "Carmen"   The very skilfully adapted libretto of the opera is the joint production of Henry Meilhac and Ludovic Halévy.   The action is animated, well-knit, and flowing, never dragging or becoming tiresome.   And it was a most masterly stroke to introduce the character of *Micaela*, which is not found in Mérimée's tale, into the play as a contrast and foil to that of *Carmen*, and in motivation of *Don José's* irresolution:—*Micaela*, the simple, true-hearted village maid,—*Carmen*, the passionate, artful, fickle Gypsy-girl.   An opportunity for musical characterization was thus presented, which the gifted composer has made one of the most attractive and effective features in a work replete with charming and striking musical effects. Bizet, well acquainted with Spanish folk-life and folk-music through frequent sojourn in the Pyrenees, portrays scenes and personages in the magical light of real "local color"—a phrase (and effect) too often misused by mediocrity.   His melody is his own.   The leading character, *Carmen*, occupies the foreground, dramatically and musically, whenever she is on the stage ; yet the lesser rôles are so carefully handled that there is no sense of disproportion.   The total effect is that of a grand art-work, cunningly wrought in the least details ; an imperishable monument to one of the greatest among modern French composers.

Index.

***

Carmen.

English version by Ruth and Thomas Martin

Nº 1. Prelude.

GEORGES BIZET.

Allegro giocoso. (♩ = 116.)

Piano.

12117

Act I.

A square in Sevilla. On the right, the door of the tobacco-factory.
At the back, a real bridge. On the left, a guard-house.
When the curtain rises, Corporal Morales and the soldiers are discovered, grouped in front of the guard-house. People coming and going on the square.

№ 2. Scene and Chorus.

TENORS.

p leggieramente.

Sur la pla - ce, Cha - cun pas - se, Cha - cun vient, cha - cun va;
La - zy peo - ple, cra - zy peo - ple, Old and young, Bold and shy,

BASSES.

Sur la pla - ce Cha - cun pas - se, Cha - cun vient, cha - cun va;
La - zy peo - ple, cra - zy peo - ple, Old and young, Bold and shy,

Drô - les de gens que ces gens là!
Stroll - ing a - long or hus - tling by,

Drô - les de gens que ces gens là!
Stroll - ing a - long or hus - tling by,

Drô - les de gens que ces gens là!
No - bod - y knows the reason why.

Drô - les de gens!
No - bod - y knows,

Drô - les de gens que ces gens là!
No - bod - y knows the reason why.

Drô - les de gens!
No - bod - y knows,

8

si - te.
coach - ing.

A son se - cours il faut al - ler! __
You do it, then, go to her aid! __

A son se - cours il faut al - ler! __
You do it, then, go to her aid! __

(to Micaela, gallantly.)

Que cher - chez - vous la bel -
Young la - dy, may I help

Micaela. (with simplicity.)   **Morales.** (with emphasis.)

le? Moi, je cherche un bri - ga - dier. Je suis là. Voi - là!
you? Yes, I'd like to speak to a guard. You're in luck, I'm here!

Micaela.

Mon bri - ga - dier à moi s'ap - pel - le Don Jo - sé. __ le con - nais - sez -
No, I am look - ing for a soldier named Don Jo - sé. __ Do you know him,

pla - ce - ra La gar - de des - cen - dan - te.
com - pa - ny will come and we'll be go - ing.

pla - ce - ra La gar - de des - cen - dan - te.
com - pa - ny will come and we'll be go - ing.

pla - ce - ra La gar - de des - cen - dan - te.
com - pa - ny will come and we'll be go - ing.

Poco ritenuto. (♩ = 88.)
(very gallantly.)

Mais en at - ten -
But may I sug -

dant qu'il vien - ne, Vou - lez - vous, la belle en - fant,
gest at pre - sent, Since you have to wait, my dear,

Vou - lez - vous pren - dre la pei - ne D'en - trer chez nous un ins -
You will find it far more pleas - ant In - side the guardhouse than out

(the soldiers surround Micaela, who tries to evade them.)

Morales.

№ 3. Chorus of Street-boys.

(The relief appears:

first a bugler and fifer, then a crowd of street-boys. __ Following the latter, Lieutenant Zuniga and

Corporal Don José, then the dragoons. __ During Street-boys' Chorus, the relief forms in front of the

guard going off duty.)

f ben ritmato, quasi staccato.

A - vec la gar - de mon-tan-te, Nous ar - ri-vons, nous voi - là!_ Son - ne, trom-
We are sol-diers marching proudly, Here we come to change the guard. Boys, blow your

petfe é-cla-tan- te! Ta ra ta ta ta ra ta ta. Nous mar-chons la tê-te hau-te
bu-gles_ loud-ly! See us march in per-fect man-ner,

Com - me de pe - tits sol - dats, Mar - quant sans fai - re de fau - te,
We are nev-er out of step. Fol - low the wav-ing_ ban-ner,

ta,— ta ra ta ta ra ta ta, ta ra ta ta ra ta ta ra ta ta ra ta ta ra

ta ta ra ta ta ra ta; — **ff** Ta ra ta ta ra ta ta,— ta ra ta ta ra ta ta, ta ra

mf unis.
ta ta ra ta ta ra ta ta ra ta ta ra ta ta ra ta ta. — Nous mar-chons la
See us march in

tê-te haute Com-me de pe-tits sol-dats, Mar-quant sans fai-
per-fect man-ner, We are nev-er out of step, Fol-low-ing the

(spoken.)
re de faute, Une, deux, mar-quant le pas. Les é-pau-les
wav-ing ban-ner, One two, one two, hep, hep. Straight in line be-

en ar-riè-re Et la poi-tri-ne en de-hors,__ Les bras de cet-
side our neigh-bors, Shoul-ders back,__ heads up high.__ We pre-sent our

te ma-niè-re, Tom-bant tout le long du corps. Nous ar-ri-vons!
trust-y sa-bers, And sa-lute you go-ing by. Com-pa-ny halt!

Nous voi-là! Ta ra ta ta ra ta tara ta ta ta ta,____ ta ra ta ta.
Stand at ease!

Recit.
Morales.

U_ne jeu-ne fil_le char-man-te Vient de nous de-man-
I have a mes-sage for you from a young and charm-ing

der si tu n'é-tais pas là! Ju_pe bleue et nat-te tom-
girl who asked to speak to you. Light blue skirt and ver-y long

Don José.

Ce doit ê - tre Mi - ca - ë - la!
I am sure that was Mi - ca - e - la.

ban - te.
braids.

(Exeunt guard going off duty. — Street-boys march off behind bugler and fifer of the retiring guard, in the same manner as they followed those of the relief.)

Et la gar - de des-cendan-te Ren-tre chez elle
We are sol - diers march-ing proud-ly, Leav-ing with the

et s'en va.— Son - ne, trom - pette é-cla-tan-te! Ta ra ta ta ta
chang-ing guard. Boys, blow your bu - gles— loud-ly!

ra ta ta. Nous mar-chons la tê - te hau - te Com - me de pe-
See us march in per-fect man-ner, We are nev - er

(spoken.)

tits sol - dats, Mar - quant sans fai - re de fau - te, Une, deux, mar -
out of step. Fol - low the wav - ing _ ban - ner, One two, one

quant le pas. Ta ra ta ta ra ta ta, _ ta ra ta ta ra ta ta
two, hep, hep!

ta, ta ra ta ta ra ta ta ra ta ta ra ta ta ra ta ta ra ta ta

ta, ta ra ta ta ra ta ta _ ta ra ta ta ra ta ta, ta ra

ta ta ra ta ta ra ta ta ra ta ta ra ta ta ra ta ta. _

Nº 3ᵇⁱˢ Recitative.

Ju - pe bleue et nat - te tom - ban - te.
"Light blue skirt and ver - y long braids!"

Don José.

Tu ne ré - ponds rien__ à ce - la? Je ré - ponds que c'est
Well, am I right__ a - bout that? I ad - mit you are

vrai, je ré - ponds que je l'ai - me!
right. I con - fess, she's the girl I love.

Recit.

Quant aux ou - vri - è - res d'i - ci, Quant__ à leur beau-
And as for the fac - to - ry girls, When__ you hear the

té, les voi - ci! Et vous pou - vez ju - ger vous - mê - me.
bell, they'll be here. Then you can judge their looks quite well.

attacca subito.

№ 4. Chorus of Cigarette-girls.

Carmen.

Sopranos I & II.
(*Cigarette-girls*).

Tenors.
(*Young men*).

Basses.
(*Townspeople*)

(The factory-bell is ringing.)

(*Don José sits down and pays no attention to the shifting scenes. He repairs the*

Piano.

chain of his saber.)

(the bell stops.) *cresc. molto.*

Allegretto moderato.

TENORS. *p leggieramente.*

La cloche a son - né;___ nous, des ouv - ri - è - res, Nous ven-ons i -
Ev-'ry day at noon,___ you will find us here,___ Wait-ing for the

ci guet - ter le re - tour; Et nous vous sui - vrons,___
time when the girls ap - pear. Charm-ing to the eye,___

bru - nes ci - ga - riè - res, En vous mur - mu - rant___ des pro - pos d'a -
how we love to court them, Hop-ing that our fond___ wish-es may come

mour!___ En vous mur - mu - rant___ des pro - pos d'a - mour!___
true,___ Hop-ing that our fond___ wish - es may come true,___

des pro - pos d'a - mour!___ des pro - pos d'a - mour!___
As all lov - ers do,___ As all lov - ers do.___

Andantino. ($\,$.$=$ 60.)

BASSES. (Enter Cigarette-girls, smoking cigarettes, and slowly descending to the stage.)

les!___ re - gards im - pu - dents,___ Mi - ne co -
are,___ the bright - eyed co - quettes,___ Keen and au -

quet - te! Fu - mant tou - tes, du bout des dents___
da - cious, I - dly smok - ing their cig - a - rettes,___

La ci - ga - ret - - - te.
And so flir - ta - - - tious!

Allegretto molto. (♩.= 108.)

BASSES.

Mais nous ne voyons   pas
But where's Carmen to-day?

Allegro moderato. (♩=92.)
(Entrance of Carmen.)

Carmen.

quasi Recit.
mf gaily (after a swift glance at Don José.)

Quand je vous ai - me - rai? ma foi, je ne sais
When I'll give you my love? Who knows, it's hard to

colla voce. *a tempo Andantino.* *colla voce.*

a tempo.

pas, Peut - ê - tre ja - mais! peut - ê - tre de -
tell! Per - haps ___ not at all. Per - haps ___ ver - y

(resolutely.)

main. Mais pas au - jour -
soon! But one thing I'll

d'hui ___ c'est cer - tain.
say: ___ Not to - day.

attacca.

Nº 5. Habanera.*)

*) Imitated from a Spanish song.

l'au-tre que je pré - fè - re Il n'a rien dit;___ mais il me
deft- ly slips through your fin-gers, For love's a thing__ no__ force can

espress.

plait.___ L'a - mour!_____ l'a -
hold.___ That's love_____ for

Sopr. *pp legg.*
L'a-mour est un oi-seau re- bel - le Que nul ne peut ap-pri-voi-
Love is free as the way-ward breeze, It can be shy, it__ can be

Ten.
L'a-mour est un oi-seau re- bel - le Que nul ne peut ap-pri-voi-
Love is free as the way-ward breeze, It can be shy, it can be

mour!_____ l'a - - mour!_____ l'a -
you, ___ That's love_____

ser, Et c'est bien en vain qu'on l'ap- pel - le S'il lui con -
bold. Love can fas - ci - nate, love can tease,___ Its whims and

ser, Et c'est bien en vain qu'on l'ap- pel - le S'il lui con -
bold. Love can fas - ci - nate, love can tease,___ Its whims and

l'a - mour! L'amour est en - fant de Bo - hême, Il n'a ja-
for you! A heart in love is quick-ly burned, It knows no

vient de re - fu - ser!
moods are thou - sand - fold.

vient de re - fu - ser!
moods are thou - sand - fold.

mais, jamais connu de loi, Si tu ne m'ai - mes pas, je t'ai - me; Si
law ex - cept its own de - sire. If I should love you and you spurn me, I'm

je t'aime, prends garde à toi! Si tu ne m'ai - mes pas, si
warning you, you play with fire! If I'm in love with you, don't

Prends garde à toi!
You play with fire!

Prends garde à toi!
You play with fire!

t'ai - me, prends garde à toi!
love you, you play with fire.

à toi!
with fire.

à toi!
with fire.

L'oiseau que tu croy - ais sur - prendre Battit de l'aile et s'en vo -
Wait for love and you wait for - ev - er, Don't wait at all, it comes to

la; L'amour est loin, tu peux l'at - ten - dre; Tu ne l'at - tends plus, il est
you. Try to grasp it, It's far too clev - er, It flies a - way in - to the

loi, Si tu ne m'ai-mes pas, je t'ai - me; Si je t'ai-me prends garde à
sire. If I should love you and you spurn _ me, I'm warning you, you play with

fant _____ de Bo - hê -
love _____ is quick - - ly

Carmen.

p

Si tu ne m'ai - mes pas. Si
If I'm in love with you, don't

f

toi! Prends garde à toi!
fire! You play with fire!

f

me! Prends garde à toi!
burned. You play with fire!

Nº 6. Scene.

56

Andante moderato. ($\quad$=58.)

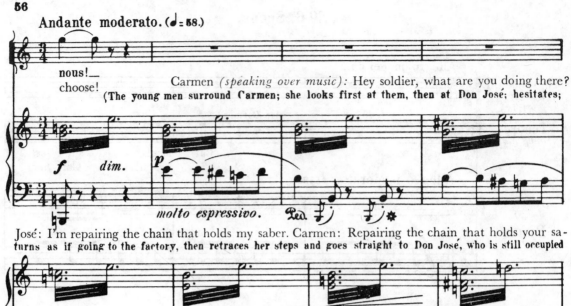

nous!__
choose!

Carmen *(speaking over music):* Hey soldier, what are you doing there?
(The young men surround Carmen; she looks first at them, then at Don José; hesitates;

José: I'm repairing the chain that holds my saber. Carmen: Repairing the chain that holds your sa-
turns as if going to the factory, then retraces her steps and goes straight to Don José, who is still occupied

ber? Really, is that *all* you want to hold? Look! Here's something to hold on to!
with his primer.__ Carmen takes from her bodice a bunch of cassia-flowers, and throws it at Don José! (This

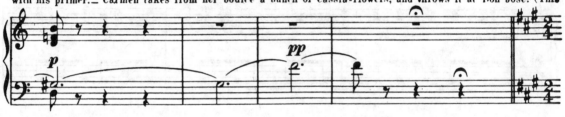

SOPRANOS.

(lightly, gathering around Don José.)
p (laughingly.)

Allegretto.($\quad$=80) *Poco più animato.*
action on this chord.) Carmen runs away; exit.)

L'a-mour est en-fant de Bo-
A heart in love is quick-ly

hême, Il n'a ja - mais, ja-mais con-nu de loi; Si tu ne
burned, It knows no law ex-cept its own de - sire, If I should

12117

m'ai - mes pas, je t'ai - me! Si je t'ai - me, prends garde à
love you and you spurn ___ me, I'm warn-ing you, you play with

Andantino, quasi Allegretto. (♩ = 104.)

(general burst of laughter)

toi! ___
fire! ___

(The factory-bell again begins to ring. Exeunt Workingmen, Young Men, etc. — The

Soldiers enter guard-house. Don José is left alone; he picks up the flowers, which had fallen at his feet.)

Nº 6bis Recitative.

Don José.

Quels re-gards! quelle effron - te - ri - e!
What out-ra-geous, scan-da-lous be - hav-iour!

Piano.

Cet - te fleur là m'a fait l'ef - fet D'u - ne bal -
And the way she threw that flow-er at me.

- le qui m'ar - ri - vait!
— It came like a dart!

Andante moderato.

Le par-fum en est fort et la fleur est jo - li - e!
But its fra-grance is sweet and the flow-er is love - ly.

Et la fem — me... S'il est vrai-
And the wom — an... if it is

ment des sor - ciè - res, C'en est u — ne cer - tai - ne —
true there are witch-es, she is one. There can be no

Allegro.   **Micaela.**   **Don José.**

ment. Jo — sé!___ Mi - ca - ë - la!
doubt. Jo — sé!___ What a sur - prise!

Micaela.   **Don José.**

Me voi - ci! Quelle joi - e!
There you are! Mi - ca - e - la!

Micaela.

C'est vo - tre mè — re qui m'en voi - e!
I bring a mes — sage from your moth-er!

attacca subito.

Nº 7. Duet.

Micaela. *rit.* *a tempo.*

puis? Et puis vraiment je n'o - se! Et puis, et puis en-
on, And then... How can I tell you.... And then, I al - so

core une au-tre cho - se Qui vaut mieux que l'ar - gent,
have an - oth - er mes-sage Which is of great-er worth,

Don José.

Et qui pour un bon fils Au - ra sans doute plus de prix. Cette au-tre
And, for a lov-ing son, Means more than all the gold on earth. That oth-er

Micaela.

cho - se, quelle est - el - le? Par - le donc! Oui je par - le - rai.
mes-sage from my moth-er, won't you say? You shall have it, too.

Ce que l'on m'a don - né, Je vous le don - ne - rai.
I prom-ised to o - bey. I'll pass it on to you.

P rit. molto. *a tempo.*

Poco più lento. (♩ = 69.)

Vo - tre mère a - vec moi sor-tait de la cha - pel - le, Et c'est a -
Aft - er church I was walk-ing home-ward with your moth-er, When she em -

lors qu'en m'embras - sant:____ Tu vas, m'a-t-elle dit, t'en al -
braced me like her own child.____ "My dear," she said to me, "Make a

legg.. ma
espr. p   Allegro moderato. (♩ = 92)

ler à la vil - le: La rou - te n'est pas lon - gue, u - ne fois a Sé -
trip to Se - ville.____ You don't have far to trav-el, And once you reach the

vil - le Tu cherche-ras mon fils, mon Jo - sé, mon en - fant!__ Tu
cit - y You'll go and find your way to Jo - sé,__ my dear son.__ You'll

dim.   rit.   Poco meno mosso. (♩ = 88)
                                                p espr.

cherche-ras mon fils,__ mon Jo - sé, mon en - fant!____ Et
go and find my son,__ my be - lov - ed Jo - sé.____ Then

colla voce.

66

cœur___ de___ for - ce et de cou - ra - ge
strong.___ His___ soul___ re-stored with cour - age.

cœur___ de___ for - ce et de cou - ra - ge.
strong.___ My___ soul___ re-stored with cour - age.___

Ô sou-ve-nirs ché - ris! Sa mère, il la re-voit, il re-voit son vil-
His heart is all a - glow As he re-calls his home and his be-lov-ed

Ô sou-ve-nirs ché - ris! Ma mè - re, je la vois, je re-vois mon vil-
My heart is all a - glow As I re-call my home and my be-lov-ed

Poco più lento.

la - - ge!___
moth - - er.___

la - - ge!___
moth - - er.___

Poco più lento. ($\quad$ = 69.)

colla voce.

Don José.

Qui sait de quel dé - mon jal - lais ê - - tre la proie!___
Who knows what turn of fate might have shat - - tered my hopes?___

12117

pp senza rigore.

Parlons de toi,— la mes-sa - gè-re; Tu vas re-tour-ner au pa-
Let's speak of you,— dear Mi-ca - e - la. When do you in-tend to go

pp *colla voce.*

Allegro moderato. (♩ = 88.)

Micaela.

ys?— Oui, ce soir mê - me: de-main je ver-rai— vo-tre
home?— Soon, this ver-y eve - ning. To - mor-row I'll be— with your

mè - - re!
moth - - er.

(animatedly.) **dim.**

Tu la verras! Eh bien! tu lui di-ras:—
I am so glad! And please, tell her for me:—

pp espress.

Que son fils l'aime et la vé - nè - - re Et qu'il se re-pent au-jour-
Tell her my thoughts are al-ways near her, And say I re-pent what I've

pp

la - ge! Il te re - voit ___ ô mon vil - la - ge! Doux souve -
moth - er. As you re - call ___ your home and moth-er Through all the

la - ge! Je te re - vois ___ ô mon vil - la - ge! Doux souve -
moth - er. As I re - call ___ my home and moth-er Through all the

(♩ = 92.)

nirs, sou - ve - nirs du pa - ys! ___ Vous rem - plis - sez son cœur de cou -
years so near and dear to you. ___ Your hope is bright, and re - stored with

nirs, sou - ve - nirs du pa - ys! ___ Vous rem - plis - sez mon cœur de cou -
years so near and dear to me. ___ My hope is bright, and re - stored with

ra - ge, Ô sou - ve - nirs, ô sou - ve - nirs ché - ris.
cour - age As you re - call your vil - lage and your home.

ra - ge, Ô sou - ve - nirs, ô sou - ve - nirs ché - ris. Je re - vois mon vil -
cour - age As I re - call my vil - lage and my home. My dear be - lov - ed

sempre **pp**

Nº 7bis Recitative.

Don José.

Res - te - là main - te - nant, pendant que je li -
Let me see what she wrote, while you stay here with

Micaela.

rai. Non pas, li - sez d'a-bord, et puis_ je re - vien - drai.
me. Oh no, I'd rath-er go, and lat-er, I will come back.

Don José.

Pour-quoi t'en al -
But why should you

Micaela.

ler? C'est plus sa - ge, Ce - la me convient da - van - ta - ge.
go? I'd pre-fer it. I'd rath-er you read it with-out me.

Li - sez! puis je re - vien - drai.
Good-bye, _ un - til lat - er on.

Don José.

Tu re - vien - dras?_
You won't be long?_

Micaela.

Je re - vien
Not long at

(exit Micaela.)

drai!
all.

Don José. *(reading):*

Ne crains rien, ma mè - re,   ton fils t'o - bé - i - ra, __ Fe-
I'll o - bey, dear moth-er,   You need not be a - fraid. __ O-

ra   ce que tu lui   dis; __   j'ai - me Mi - ca - ë - la, Je la prendrai pour
bey   with a hap-py heart. __   I   give my sol-emn word to mar-ry Mi - ca-

poco rit.

fem - - - - me, Quant à tes   fleurs __ sorcière in - fâ - me!...
e - - - - la,   In spite of   you, __ you and your flow - ers.

poco rit.

attacca subito.

12117

№ 8. Chorus.

SOPRANOS I. (on stage.)

Au secours! au secours! n'en - ten - dez-vous pas?
Hur-ry up, hur-ry up. Can't some - bod - y hear?

SOPRANOS II.

(on stage.)

Au secours! au secours! messieurs les sol - dats!
Hur-ry up, hur-ry up! Some-one in - ter - fere!

C'est la Car-men-ci - ta!
Car - men be - gan the fight!

Non, non, ce n'est pas el - le!
No, no, she did - n't do it!

C'est la Carmen-ci - ta!
Car - men be - gan the fight!

C'est el - le!
She did it!

Non, non ce n'est pas el - le! pas du
No, no, she did - n't do it! Not at

78

SOPRANOS II.
(drawing Zuniga to their side.)

La Ma - nue - li - ta di - sait,___ Et ré - pé - tait à voix
This is how it came to pass:___ When Ma - nu - e - la kept

hau - - te Quel - le a - chè - te - rait sans fan - te
talk - - ing That she had e - nough of walk - ing

SOPRANOS I.
(same business.)

Un â - ne qui lui plai - sait.___ A - lors la Car - men - ci -
She would go and buy an ass.___ Car - men shout - ed through the

ta___ Rail - leuse à son or - di - nai - re,
room,___ (May - be she tried to be fun - ny):

Dit: "Un â - ne pour-quoi fai - - - re? Un ba - lai te suf - fi -
"You would on - ly waste your mon - - ey, You'd look bet - ter on a

SOPRANOS II.

ra." Ma-nue-li-ta ri-pos - ta Et dit a sa ca-ma-
broom!" Ma-nu-e - la shout-ed back: "You cat, you are on - ly

ra - de: "Pour cer-tai - ne pro - me - na - de, Mon
jeal - ous. You don't e - ven have to tell us, We

SOPRANOS I.

â - ne te ser-vi - ra! Et ce jour la tu pour-
know all your gyp-sy pack!" "You can't buy a pair of

ras A bon droit fai-re la fiè - re, Deux la-quais sui-vront der-
shoes, Let a - lone don-keys to ride on, So why put that air of

84

12117

Nº 9. Song and Melodrama.

90

12117

Zuniga.

C'est dom-ma - ge,
It's a shame, though,

C'est grand dom-ma - ge,
She's such a wild - cat!

Car elle est gen-
For she has

til - le vràiment:
spir - it and wit!

Mais il faut
But we must

ppp

bien la ren - dre sa - ge,
tame her just a bit.

At - ta -
Tie her

chez ces deux jo - lis bras.
hands be - hind her back!

Recit.

Carmen

Où me con-dui -rez- vous?
Where are you go-ing to take me?

Don José.

A la pri - son et je n'y puis rien fai - re.
You go to jail, and no one can pre-vent it.

Carmen.

Vraiment tu n'y peux rien fai - re.
In - deed, no one can pre - vent it?

Don José.

Non, rien! j'o- bé - is à mes
That's right. I must do as I'm

chefs. Eh bien moi, je sais bien qu'en dé - pit de tes chefs eux-
told. E - ven so, I will bet that no mat-ter how strict the

mê - mes Tu fe - ras tout ce que je veux, Et ce - la, par-ce - que tu
or - der You will help me to es - cape. You know why? Be-cause you

Don Jose. Carmen.

m'aimes. Moi t'ai-mer! Oui, Jo-sé! La fleur dont je t'ai fait pré-sent __ Tu
love me. I, love you? Yes, Jo-sé! The flow-er I gave you to-day, __ the

sais, __ la fleur de la sor-cière, Tu peux la je-ter main-te-
flow-er you hid there in your jack et, you might as well throw it a-

Allegro. **Don Jose.**

nant, Le charme o-pè-re! Ne me par-le plus, Tu m'en-
way, it has done its du-ty. You're go-ing too far! Once for

Moderato.

tends? Ne par-le plus, Je le dé-fends.
all, you must not talk. That's a com-mand.

Carmen *(speaking over music):*
Very well, General, very

well! You forbid me to talk, so I won't talk.

№ 10. Seguidilla and Duet.

la Sé - gue - dille Et boi - re du Man - za - nil - la.
dance Se - gui - dil - la And to drink Man - za - nil - la,

J'i - rai chez mon a - mi Lil - las Pas - tia.
At the inn of Se - nor Lil - las Pas - tia.

sempre pp

sempre pp

Oui, mais tou - te seule
But when a girl goes

on s'en - nui - e, Et les vrais plai - sirs sont à deux;
there to dance, She wants to have some com - pa - ny.

Moderato, quasi recitativo.

Don José. (with severity.)

Tais - toi! je t'a - vais dit ___ de ne pas me par -
E - nough! For the last time ___ I for - bid you to

fp colla voce.

a tempo. (♩=84.)

Carmen. (with simplicity.)

ler! Je ne te par - le pas, je chan - te pour moi -
talk. I do not talk to you. I sing for my own

poco ritenuto.

mê - me, je chan - te pour moi - mê - me! Et je
plea - sure, I sing for my own plea - sure. And I'm

a tempo.

pen - se! il n'est pas dé - fen - du de pen -
think - ing! And ev - 'ry - bod - y knows thoughts are

104

12117

la Sé - gue - dille Et boi - rons du Man - za -
dance Se - gui - dil - la And we'll drink Man - za -

nil - la: _____
nil - la. _____

sempre f

tra la la la

la la la la la la la, _____ tra la

la la la la la la la la la la.

attacca subito.

N⁰ 11. Finale.

(making a backward gesture with her head)

rai,   je te pousse - rai___ Aussi fort que je le pour-
way.   Stay in back of me, ___ And I'll give you a heav-y

rai,   Lais-se - toi ren - ver - ser...
push.   Turn a - round as you fall.

(They begin to march off.)

Le res- -te me - re - gar- -de.
The rest I will take care of.

Allegretto quasi Andantino. (♩ = 72.)

Carmen. (singing, and laughing in Zuniga's face.)

L'a-mour est en-fant de Bo - hême, Il n'a ja - mais, jamais connu de
A heart in love is quick-ly burned, It knows no law ex - cept its own de -

sempre pp

12117

loi; Si tu ne m'aimes pas, je t'ai-me; Si je t'ai-me,prends garde à
sire. If I should love you and you spurn me, I'm warn-ing you, you play with

toi!___ Si tu ne m'aimes pas, si tu ne m'aimes pas, je
fire!___ If I'm in love with you, Don't ev-er, ev-er try to

cresc. - - - - *f*

t'ai-me! Mais si je t'ai-me, si je t'ai-me prends garde à___
spurn me. My friend, re-mem-ber, if I love_you, you play with_

(she marches off with Don José and the Soldiers.)

toi!
fire.

sempre
pp

Allegro vivace. ($\textit{d}$=92.)

(At the bridge, Carmen pushes José. He falls and she escapes, laughing loudly.)

ff

(General laugh.)

(Curtain.)

tutta forza.

End of Act I.

Entr' acte.

Allegro moderato. ($\quad = 100.$)

Piano.

Act II.

Lillas Pastia's Inn. When the curtain rises, Carmen, Frasquita, and Mercedes are discovered seated at a table with the officers. Dance of the Gypsy-girls, accompanied by Gypsies playing the guitar and tambourine.

№ 12. Gypsy Song.

ben ritmato.

Carmen. (Gypsy Song.)

(The dance ceases.)

Les
The

tringles des sistres tin - taient_____ A - vec un é - clat mé - tal -
still-ness at the end of day _____ Is bro-ken by a la-zy

li - que, Et sur cette é-tran-ge mu - si - que Les__
jin - gle, The sleep-y air be-gins to tin - gle. The__

Zin - ga-rel-las se le - vaient.____ Tam-
gyp - sy dance is un-der way._____ And

bours de Bas-que allaient leur train, Et les gui - ta-res for-ce-
soon the tam-bou-rines of Spain, And strumming of gui-tars com-

116

12117

Frasquita, Mercedes.

tra la la la, _____ tra la la la, _____

tra la la la, _____ tra la la la, _____

tra la la la, _____ tra la la la la la la la la. _____

tra la la la, _____ tra la la la la la la la. _____

(Dance.)

(The dance ceases.)

sempre **p**

Les
The

anneaux de cuivre et d'ar - gent _____ Re - lui-saient sur les peaux bi -
cop - per rings the gyp - sies wèar _____ A - gainst their dusk - y skins are

la,   tra la la   la,   tra

la,   tra la la   la,   tra

la la la la la la   la.

la la la la la la   la.

cresc.

(The dance ceases.)

Les   Bo-hémiens à tour de   bras   De
The   gyp - sy men play on with fire,   Their

leurs in-struments faisaient   ra - ge,   Et   cet é-blou-is-sant ta-
tam-bou - rines are loud-ly   whir - ring.   The   pul-sing rhy-thm fierce-ly

pa - ge En - sor - ce - lait les Zin - ga - ras.
stir - ring En - flames the gyp - sy girls' de - sire.

Sous le rythme de la chan - son,
Their pas - sion car - ries them a - way,

Sous le rythme de la chan -
Their ag - ile bod - ies turn and

son,
sway

Ar - den - tes, fol - les, en - fié - vré - - es, El - les
In burn - ing fren - zy and a - ban - don. On and

se lais - saient, en - i - vré - - es, Em - por - ter par le tour - bil -
on they dance - mad - ly driv - en Like a whirl - wind no force can

tutta forza.

Ped.

sec.

№ 12 bis. Recitative.

Nº 13. Chorus.

vat!_____
rah!_____

vat!_____
rah!_____

vat!_____
rah!_____

vat!_____
rah!_____

vat!_____
rah!_____

vat!_____
rah!_____

№ 14 . Couplets.

*) In case the part of Carmen, in the ensembles of the second and third acts, is too low for the voice
of the artist taking that rôle, she may sing the part of Frasquita or Mercedes.
12117

mour t'at - tend, To - ré - a - dor, L'a-mour, l'a - mour t'at - -
ri - ta's love, To - re - a - dor, your sweet re - ward is

mour, L'a-mour, l'a - mour t'at -
ward, your sweet re - ward is

mour, L'a-mour, l'a - mour t'at - -
prize, your sweet re - ward is

To - ré - a - dor! L'a-mour, l'a - mour t'at -
To - re - a - dor, your sweet re - ward is

mour, L'a-mour, l'a - mour t'at - -
ward, your sweet re - ward is

mour, t'at -
ward is

t'at - tend, oui, l'a - mour t'at -
love, To - re - a - dor, is

len - ce... on fait si - len - ce... Ah! que se passe-t-il?___
si - lent. What are they waiting for, And what is hap-pen-ing?___

Plus de cris, c'est l'instant! Plus de cris, c'est l'instant!
Breathless ex - pect - an - cy Hush - es the gal - ler - y.

Le tau - reau s'é - lance En bon - dis - sant hors du To - ril!___
Through the gate the bull is leap - ing out in - to the ring!___

Il s'é - lan - ce! il en-tre, il frap - pe!___ un che - val
Rush - ing on,___ he charg - es mad - ly.___ A horse goes

Nº 14 bis. Recitative.

Escamillo.

Cet - te ré - pon - se n'est pas ten - dre,
That does not sound ver - y in - vit - ing.

Je me con - ten -
And I've no oth - er

rai d'es - pé - rer et d'at - ten - dre.
choice but to hope and keep wait - ing.

Carmen.

Il est per - mis d'at -
I can't stop you from

ten - dre. il est doux d'es - pé - rer.
wait - ing, and to hope is al - ways sweet.

Zuniga.

Puis - que tu ne viens pas, Car -
Since you have de - cid - ed to

men. je re - vien - drai.
stay, I shall come back.

Carmen.

Et vous au - rez grand tort!
That would be a mis - take!

Zuniga.

Bah! je me ris - que - rai.
Bah! That risk I will take!

Escamillo *(spoken):* My friends, I thank you all.

N⁰ 14ᵗᵉʳ. Exit of Escamillo.

Allegro moderato. (♩ = 108.)

№ 14 ^{quater}. Recitative.

Frasquita.
Eh bien vi - te, quel - les nou - vel -
Tell us quick-ly, what are you plan -

El Dancairo.
les? Pas trop mau-vai - ses les nou - vel - les, Et nous pou-vons en
ning? We're han-dling goods com-ing from Eng-land. I'm sure we'll get them

cor fai - re quel - ques beaux coups, Mais nous a -
through in the u - su - al way. But you three

Frasq., Merc., Carmen.
Be-soin de nous?
We'll go a - long?

vons be-soin de vous... Oui, nous a-vons be-soin de vous.
girls must go a - long. I must be sure noth-ing goes wrong.

Nᵒ 15. Quintet.

156

12117

vou - ons hum - ble - ment:_____

needs a wom - an's touch._____

pp legg.

Quand il s'a-git de trom-pe-ri-e, De du-pe-ri-e, De vo-le-ri-e,

When it's a case of dou - ble deal-ing, Ly - ing or steal-ing, Bet-ter concealing,

pp

Il est toujours bon, sur ma foi, D'avoir les fem - mes a-vec soi.

It hap-pens time and time a-gain, Wom-en are more sub - tle than men.

El Remendado.

Et sans el-les, Mes toutes bel-les, On ne fait ja-mais rien De bien!

In ad - di - tion, Their in - tu - i - tion Can turn a guess to sure suc-cess!

El Dancaïro.

Et sans el-les, Mes toutes bel-les, On ne fait ja-mais rien De bien!

In ad - di - tion, Their in - tu - i - tion Can turn a guess to sure suc-cess!

(Carmen exchanges with Mercedes to the last measure on page 166.)

Les tou-tes bel-les, On ne fait ja-mais rien De bien!
Their in-tu-i-tion Can turn a guess to sure suc-cess!

Les tou-tes bel-les, On ne fait ja-mais rien De bien!
Their in-tu-i-tion Can turn a guess to sure suc-cess!

Les tou-tes bel-les, On ne fait ja-mais rien De bien!
Their in-tu-i-tion Can turn a guess to sure suc-cess!

Les tou-tes bel-les, On ne fait ja-mais rien De bien!
Their in-tu-i-tion Can turn a guess to sure suc-cess!

Les tou-tes bel-les, On ne fait ja-mais rien De bien!
Their in-tu-i-tion Can turn a guess to sure suc-cess!

Oui, quand il s'a-git de trom-pe-ri-e, De du-pe-ri-e, De vo-le-
Yes, in an-y case of dou-ble deal-ing, of ly-ing, steal-ing or con-

Oui, quand il s'a-git de trom-pe-ri-e, De du-pe-ri-e, De vo-le-
Yes, in an-y case of dou-ble deal-ing, of ly-ing, steal-ing or con-

Oui, quand il s'a-git de trom-pe-ri-e, De du-pe-ri-e, De vo-le-
Yes, in an-y case of dou-ble deal-ing, of ly-ing, steal-ing or con-

Oui, quand il s'a-git de trom-pe-ri-e, De du-pe-ri-e, De vo-le-
Yes, in an-y case of dou-ble deal-ing, of ly-ing, steal-ing or con-

Oui, quand il s'a-git de trom-pe-ri-e, De du-pe-ri-e, De vo-le-
Yes, in an-y case of dou-ble deal-ing, of ly-ing, steal-ing or con-

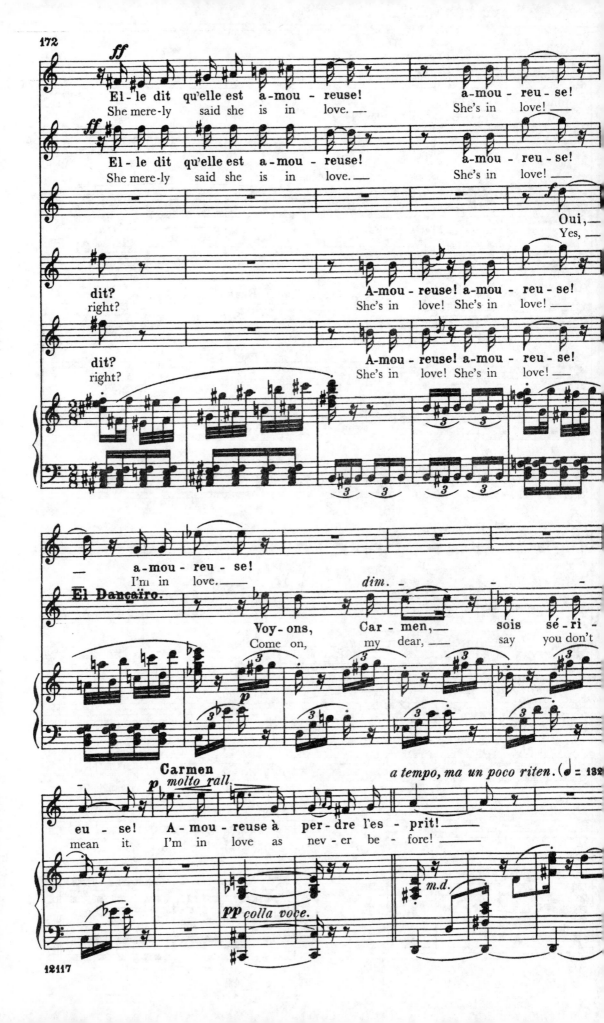

(ironicamente.)

La cho - se, cer - tes, nous é - tonne, Mais
We must ad - mit we are a - stounded, Be -

ce n'est pas le pre - mier jour Où vous au -
cause you've shown us more than once How eas - y

rez su, ma mi - gnon - ne, Fai - re mar - cher de
you have al - ways found it, To com - bine your

front le de - voir,— le de - voir et l'a -
du - ty with love.— You know well,— ver - y

mour,— Fai - re mar - cher le de - voir et l'a - mour.
well,— How to com - bine your— du - ty with love.

leggieramente.

sempre pp

mf (francamente.)

Mes a - mis, je se - rais fort
You know that I would join you

aise De par - tir a - vec vous ce
gladly In this new plan you've spo - ken

soir; Mais cet - te fois, ne vous dé -
of. Though I may dis - ap - point you

plai - se, Il fau dra que l'a -
bad - ly, Just this once love comes

mour passe a - vant le de -
first, Just this once love comes

f *p* *mf* *p* *dim.*

Nº 15ᵇⁱˢ. Recitative.

Recitative.

El Dancaïro.

Carmen.

Mais qui donc at-tends - tu? Près - que
Who is the luck - y man? If you must

Piano.

Moderato.

misurato.

rien, un sol-dat qui l'au-tre jour__ pour me ren-dre ser -
know, it's a sol-dier of the guard,__ who, in or-der to

vi - ce S'est fait mettre en pri - son. Le fait est dé - li -
help me, went to pris - on for me. A most beau-ti-ful

El Remendado.

El Dancaïro.

cat. Il se peut qu'a-près tout__ ton sol-dat ré - flé -
thought! It may be that your man__ has be-come less o-

chisse. Es-tu bien su - re qu'il vien-dra?__
blig-ing. How do you know that he will come?

Nº 16. Song
(Canzonetta.)

Allegro moderato. (♩ = 100.)

Carmen.

É-cou-

Don José. (Behind the scenes, far away.)

Hal-te-là! Qui va là? Dragon d'Alca-la!__
Who are you? Some-one new? Sol-dier, who goes there?__

tez!
hear?

Le voi-là!
I was right!

Où t'en vas-tu par là, Dra-gon d'Alca-la?__ Moi, je m'en vais
Where are you go-ing to? Sol-dier,__tell me where?__ Look-ing for my

fai-re__ mor-dre la pous-siè-re A mon ad-ver-
ri-val,__ I in-tend to meet him, Fight him and de-

sai——re. S'il en est ain-si, pas-sez, mon a-
feat——him. Since the case is so, Free-ly you may

mi.__ Af-fai-re d'hon-neur,__ Af-fai-re de
go.__ Hon-or's stern com-mand, Af-fairs of the

cœur; Pour nous tout est là,__ Dra-gons d'Al-ca-la.
heart, Those are things a-part.__ Sol-diers un-der-stand.

Recit.
Frasquita.

C'est un beau dra-gon.__
That's a hand-some boy!__

Mercedes.

Un très beau dra-gon.__
A ver-y handsome boy!__

El Dancaïro.

Qui se-rait pour
Men like that we

(Enter Don José.)

№. 16bis Recitative.

Carmen.

Allegro.   Recit.   Don José.

En - fin c'est toi!   Car -
You're here at last!   Car -

Piano.

men!   Et tu sors de pri - son?   J'y suis res - té deux
men!   You had to go to jail?   For all ____ of two

p alla misura.

Tu t'en plains?
You com - plain?

mois.   Ma foi non!   Et si c'é - tait pour
months.   Not a bit.   And, if it were for

Tu m'aimes donc?
Then you love me?

toi, j'y voudrais être en - co - re.   Moi,— je t'a -
you, they could have kept me long - er.   Love you? I a -

Attacca subito.

№ 17. Duet.

190 Allegretto. (♩ = 108.)
(dancing, and accompanying herself with the castanets.)

La____ la_ la_ la_ la____ la_ la_ la_
Castagnette.

la____ la_ la____ la_ la____ la_ la____ la_

la____ la____ la____ la_ la_ la_

la____ la____ la____ la_ la_ la_

*) *Note:* The castanet-part, printed in small notes, may be performed either in the orchestra by one of the players belonging to the latter, or on the stage by the artist singing the rôle of Carmen, in which case the rhythm may be modified at the pleasure of the artist.

bas...
hear ...

Oui,
Yes,

ce sont nos clai-rons qui son-nent la re-
our bu-gles are blow-ing, Sound-ing the re-

cresc.

Carmen.

Bra-vo! bra-vo!
Bra-vo, bra-vo!

j'avais beau fai-re; il
That's e-ven bet-ter! It's

traite; Ne les entends-tu pas?
treat. Now, don't you hear them, too?

est mé-lan-co-li-que De dan-ser sans or-chestre. Et
not an eas-y thing to sing and dance _ with-out mu-sic. But

mf *cresc.*

vi-ve la mu-si-que Qui nous tom-be du ciel!
now we have some mu-sic which has dropped from the sky.

(dancing, and rattling the castanets.)

la _____

Cast

194

Allegretto molto moderato. **ff**
(♪ = 152.)   (with an outburst.)   a piacere.   a tempo.

Ah! j'étais vraiment trop bê - te!
Ah, how could I be so stu - pid!

a tempo.

a piacere.   a tempo.

Ah! j'étais vrai-ment trop bê - te! Je me mettais en quatre et
Ah, how could I be so stu - pid! I took no end of pains, I

a tempo.

colla voce.   a tempo.

je faisais des frais, oui, je faisais des frais, Pour a - muser mon - sieur.
tried my ver - y best, my ver - y, ver - y best To en - ter-tain my guest.

rit: a tempo.
colla voce.

cresc.   3   3

Je chan - tais!   je dan - sais!   Je crois, Dieu me par -
So I sang   and I danced,   Think-ing, (may God for -

3   **f**   **p**

donne, Qu'un peu plus je l'ai - mais! Ta ra ta ta - C'est le clairon qui
give me), I was al - most in love! He hears the blast-ed

cresc.   dim.   **p**

Andantino. (♩ = 69.)

Don José.

p con amore.

La fleur que tu m'avais je - té - e, Dans ma pri-son m'é-tait res-
Through ev -'ry long and lone-ly hour ___ In pris - on there, I kept your

té - e, Flé - trie et sè - che, cet-te fleur Gardait tou-
flow - er, And though its bloom ___ was swift-ly gone Its haunt-ing

jours ___ sa douce o - deur; Et pen-dant des heu-res en-
fra - grance lin-gered on. In the dark - ness, as ___ I lay

tiè - res, Sur mes yeux, fermant mes pau - piè - res, De
dream - ing, Its per-fume, con - sol-ing, re - deem - ing, Re -

cette o‐deur_ je m'eni‐vrais
called your im‐age night and day,

Et dans la nuit_ je te vo‐
And my de‐spair_ would fade a‐

Poco animato, ma poco.

p   **cresc.**

yais!_ Je me pre‐nais_ à te mau‐di‐re, A
way._ An‐oth‐er time,_ I would be‐rate you, I

dim.   **pp**

a tempo. **p**

te dé‐tes‐ter,_ à me di‐re: Pour‐quoi faut‐il_ que le des‐
swore to de‐test_ and to hate you! Of what Nem‐e‐sis_ am I the

a tempo.   *dim.*   **p**

pp

tin_ L'ait mi‐se là_ sur mon che‐min!_____ Puis
prey?_ What whim of fate_ sent you my way?_____ Then

dim.

*) In case the part of this duet included between A and B (page 210) is too low for the voice of the artist singing the rôle of Carmen, transpose a tone higher (without transition).

Le ciel ou-vert, la vie er-ran-te; Pour pa-ys, l'u-ni-vers; Et pour loi, sa vo-lon-té! Et sur tout la chose en-i-vran-te: La li-ber-té! la li-ber-té!

Hap-py to roam the o-pen spa-ces, All the world for our home, We o-bey our will a-lone. Best of all, a price-less pos-ses-sion, Our life is free, Our life is free.

Là-bas, là-bas dans la mon-
Peo-ple in love be-long to-

Don José.
Mon Dieu!
My God!

12117

ta - gne.
geth - - er,
(in painful irresolution.)

Car - men!
O Car - men,

Là-bas, là - bas si tu m'ai
They can - not bear to be a -

mais,
part.

Tais - toi!
no more!

Là-bas, là - bas tu me sui
Car-ry me off and far a -

cresc. molto.

poco a poco cresc.

vrais! Sur ton che-val tu me pren - drais!
way, Shar-ing ad - ven-tures day by day.

Sur
If

Ah! Carmen, hé - las! tais-toi! tais-toi!
Car - men, please, no more! I beg of

mf cresc.

ton che-val tu me pren-drais Et comme un brave à tra-vers la cam-
you're in love with me, Jo - sé, You'll car-ry me a - cross the far off

toi!
you,

mon
no

Dieu!
more!

p

cresc.

Attacca.

Nº 18. Finale.

Zuniga. (enters after forcing the door.) (he perceives Don José.)

J'ou-vre moi-mê-me... et j'en-tre...
What's go-ing on here, I ask you.

(to Carmen) leggiero.

Ah!_ fi! ah! fi! la bel-le! Le choix n'est pas heu-
Oh,_ shame, my love-ly Car-men, Your taste _ is rath-er

reux! c'est se mé-sal-li-er De pren-dre le sol-dat_
poor. When there's an of-fi-cer Who of-fers so much more,_

(to Don José.) Don José. (calmly, but resolutely.)

quand on a l'of-fi-cier!_ Al-lons, dé-cam-pe! Non!
It's a pri-vate you pre-fer. _ Get out, and hur-ry! No!

Zuniga. (sternly.) Don José. Zuniga. (menacing Don José.)

Si fait!_ tu par-ti-ras! Je ne par-ti-rai pas! Drô-le!
Get out,_ there is the door! I don't in-tend to go. Scoundrel!

Allegro moderato.

Carmen. (throwing herself between them.)

mf

Au dia - ble le ja-
You're mad,— you jeal-ous

Don José. (seizing his sabre.)

ff

Ton-ner-re! il va pleu-voir des coups!
Damna - tion! I'll show you who will go!

Allegro moderato. (♩=76.)

ff   *p*

ff

loux! A moi!_____ à moi!_____
fool! Come here!_____ Come here!_____

(The Gypsies appear from every side; at a sign from Carmen, El Dancaïro and El Remendado

cresc.

seize Zuniga, and disarm him.)

f   *cresc.*

ff

216

218

12117

Frasquita and Mercedes. (Carmen exchanges with Mercedes to the end of the act.)

(to Don José.)

Suis - nous à tra - vers la cam - pa - gne, Viens a - vec
Come fol - low us in - to the mountains, Be one of

(to Don José.)

té! ____ Suis - nous a tra - vers la cam - pa - gne, Viens a - vec
free. ____ Come fol - low us in - to the mountains, Be one of

El Remendado. (to Don José.)

A - mi, suis - nous dans la cam - pa - gne,
Be one of us, and you will see

El Dancaïro. (to Don José.)

A - mi, suis - nous dans la cam - pa - gne,
Be one of us, and you will see

Chorus.

SOPRANOS I. (to Don José.)

Suis - nous à tra - vers la cam pa - gne, Viens a - vec
Come fol - low us in - to the mountains, Be one of

SOPRANOS II. (to Don José.)

TENORS. (to Don José.)

A - mi, suis - nous dans la cam - pa - gne,
Be one of us, and you will see

BASSES. (to Don José.)

sempre f

nous dans la mon - ta- -gne, Suis - nous et tu t'y fe -
us, be our com - pan - - ion. Come with us and you will

Viens a-vec nous à la mon-ta-gne, Tu t'y fe - ras,
What life can be Once you are free. Be one of us,

Viens a-vec nous à la mon-ta-gne, Tu t'y fe - ras,
What life can be Once you are free. Be one of us,

nous dans la mon - ta- -gne, Suis - nous et tu t'y fe -
us, be our com - pan - - ion. Come with us and you will

Viens a -vec nous à la mon-ta-gne, Tu t'y fe - ras,
What life can be Once you are free. Be one of us.

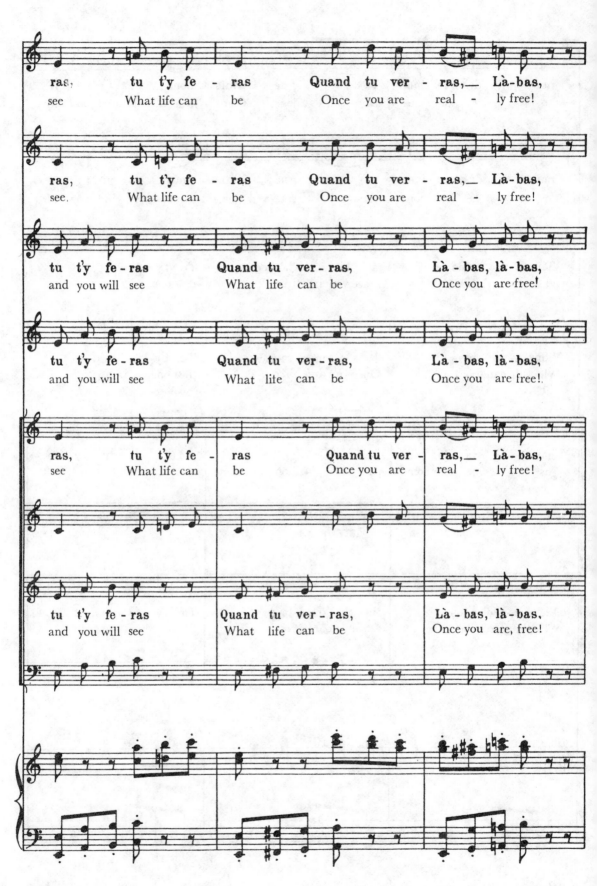

End of Act II.

Entr'acte.

Andantino, quasi Allegretto. (♩=88.)

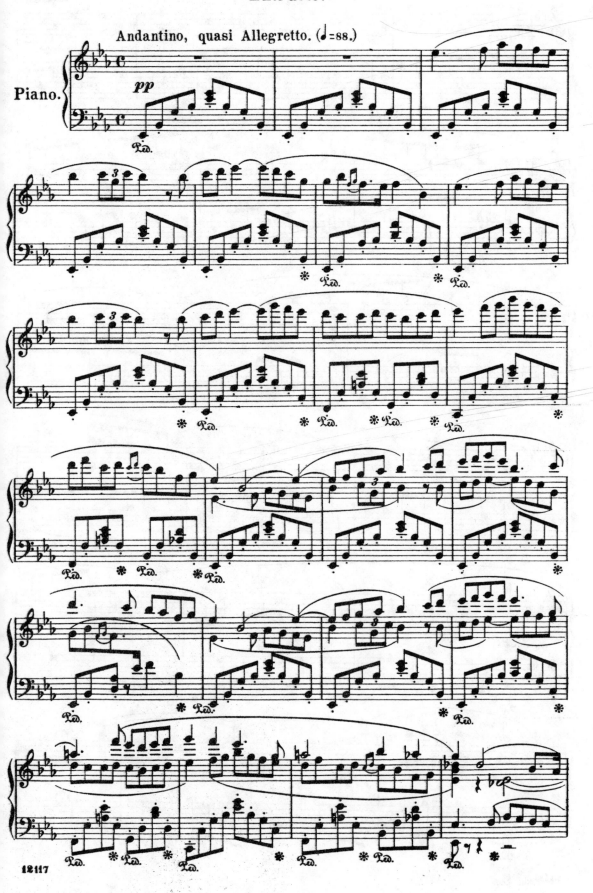

Act III.

A wild spot in the mountains.

№ 19. Sextet and Chorus.

Entry of the Gypsies.

Carmen exchanges with Mercedes (or Frasquita) to the end of this number.

Et le pé - ril,___ le pé - ril est en haut,___ il
We must be keen, ___ a - lert and un - a - fraid, ___ For

Et le pé - ril,___ le pé - ril est en haut,___ il
We must be keen, ___ a - lert and un - a - fraid, ___ For

Et le pé - ril,___ le pé - ril est en haut,___ il
We must be keen, ___ a - lert and un - a - fraid, ___ For

Et le pé - ril,___ le pé - ril est en haut,___ il
We must be keen, ___ a - lert and un - a - fraid, ___ For

Et le pé - ril,___ le pé - ril est en haut,___ il
We must be keen, ___ a - lert and un - a - fraid, ___ For

Et le pé - ril,___ le pé - ril est en haut,___ il
We must be keen, ___ a - lert and un - a - fraid, ___ For

mf.

est en bas, il est en haut, Il est par-tout, qu'impor-te!
dan - ger lies at ev-'ry turn, At ev - 'ry hour it's near us.

est en bas, il est en haut, Il est par-tout, qu'impor-te!
dan - ger lies at ev-'ry turn, At ev - 'ry hour it's near us.

est en bas, il est en haut, Il est par-tout, qu'impor-te!
dan - ger lies at ev-'ry turn, At ev - 'ry hour it's near us.

est en bas, il est en haut, Il est par-tout, qu'impor-te!
dan - ger lies at ev-'ry turn, At ev - 'ry hour it's near us.

est en bas, il est en haut, Il est par-tout, qu'impor-te!
dan - ger lies at ev-'ry turn, At ev - 'ry hour it's near us.

est en bas, il est en haut, Il est par-tout, qu'impor-te!
dan - ger lies at ev-'ry turn, At ev - 'ry hour it's near us

f

Nous al - lons___ de - vant nous___ sans sou - ci___ du tor - rent,
On _ our way, ___ un - concerned, ___ Come what may, ___ we pre - vail,

Nous al - lons___ de - vant nous___ sans sou - ci___ du tor - rent,
On _ our way, ___ un - concerned, ___ Come what may, ___ we pre - vail,

Nous al - lons___ de - vant nous___ sans sou - ci___ du tor - rent,
On _ our way, ___ un - concerned, ___ Come what may, ___ we pre - vail,

Nous al - lons___ de - vant nous___ sans sou - ci___ du tor - rent,
On _ our way, ___ un - concerned, ___ Come what may, ___ we pre - vail,

Nous al - lons___ de - vant nous___ sans sou - ci___ du tor - rent,
On _ our way, ___ un - concerned, ___ Come what may, ___ we pre - vail,

Nous al - lons___ de - vant nous___ sans sou - ci___ du tor - rent,
On _ our way, ___ un - concerned, ___ Come what may, ___ we pre - vail,

p cresc. molto.

Sans sou - ci du tor - rent, Sans sou - ci de l'o - ra - ge!
Through the haz - ard - ous storm, While the thunder is roll - ing.

Sans sou - ci du tor - rent, Sans sou - ci de l'o - ra - ge!
Through the haz - ard - ous storm, While the thunder is roll - ing.

Sans sou - ci du tor - rent, Sans sou - ci de l'o - ra - ge!
Through the haz - ardous storm, While the thunder is roll - ing.

Sans sou - ci du tor - rent, Sans sou - ci de l'o - ra - ge!
Through the haz - ardous storm, While the thunder is roll - ing.

Sans sou - ci du tor - rent, Sans sou - ci de l'o - ra - ge!
Through the haz - ardous storm, While the thunder is roll - ing.

Sans sou - ci du tor - rent, Sans sou - ci de l'o - ra - ge!
Through the haz - ardous storm, While the thunder is roll - ing.

p *cresc. molto.* *f* *ff*

248

Sans sou-ci nous al-lons en a-vant!_____ E-cou-te, é-
We will get to our goal, come what may._____ Be cau-tious, be

Sans sou-ci nous al-lons en a-vant!_____ E-cou-te, é-
We will get to our goal, come what may._____ Be cau-tious, be

Sans sou-ci nous al-lons en a-vant!_____ E-cou-te, é-
We will get to our goal, come what may._____ Be cau-tious, be

Sans sou-ci nous al-lons en a-vant!_____ E-cou-te, é-
We will get to our goal, come what may._____ Be cau-tious, be

Sans sou-ci nous al-lons en a-vant!_____ E-cou-te, é-
We will get to our goal, come what may._____ Be cau-tious, be

Sans sou-ci nous al-lons en a-vant!_____ E-cou-te, é-
We will get to our goal, come what may._____ Be cau-tious, be

SOPRANOS.

A-mi,_____ là-bas
Watch out,_____ watch out _____

TENORS.

Oui,
'Down

BASSES I.

A-mi,_____ là-bas
Watch out,_____ watch out _____

BASSES II.

Oui,
Down

18117

№ 19bis. Recitative.

Recit. **Carmen.** (to José.)

Que regardes-tu
Why do you stare like

Don José.

donc? Je me dis que là - bas Il ex - iste u - ne
that? I was think - ing that there in the valley lives a

bon-ne et bra-ve vieil - le fem-me qui me croit hon-nête homme.
kind and God - fear-ing wom - an who be - lieves me to be hon-est.

El - le se trompe, hé - las!
I have not kept her faith.

Allegro moderato.

Recit.

Carmen.

Qui donc est cet-te femme?
And who is that sweet la - dy?

Don José.

Ah! Carmen, sur mon â - me, ne raille pas —
I am warn-ing you, Carmen, watch what you say; —

Car c'est ma mè - re.
she is my moth-er.

Carmen.

Eh bien — va la re - trou-ver — tout de
I see. — Then you should go home — to your

sui - te. No - tre mé - tier, vois - tu, ne te vaut rien —
moth-er. The kind of life we lead is not for you. —

Et tu fe-rais fort bien de par-tir au plus vi - te.
And you might as well leave us, the soon - er the better.

Don José.

Par-tir, nous sé-pa-
You say that I should

alla misura.

Carmen.

rer? / leave?

Sans dou - te! / Precise - ly.

Don José.

Nous sé - pa - rer, Car- / And go away from

p espress.

men ____ / you? ____

Recit.

É - cou - te, si tu re - dis ce mot ____ / I warn you, if you say that once more...

Carmen.

Tu / You

f   *ff*

me tu erais, peut - ê - tre. / mean that you would kill me?

Quel re - gard ____ / How fierce you look. ____

p

6   6   6   6

tu ne réponds rien ____ / You don't say a word. ____

3

Que m'importe? après tout, le destin est le maître! / It is all in the cards, we have no way to change it.

p — *f*

p

№ 20. Trio.

f
Bien! c'est ce - la!
Come, let us try!
la!
try!
mf
Trois
Three
poco sf
pp
mf
Trois car - tes i - ci,
Three cards to the left.
car - tes i - ci,
cards to the right,
Qua - tre
Four a -
f
Qua - tre là!
Four be - low.
là!
bove.
poco sf
p
p

Frasquita.

Par - lez!___
Let's see!___

Mercedes.

Par - lez!___
Let's see!___

Moderato. Frasquita.

(♩. = 88)

Moi, je vois un jeune a - mou - reux, Qui m'aime on ne peut davan-
See, my man is youthful and bold, One lov - er with daring and

ta - ge:
cour - age. **Mercedes.**

Le mien est très - riche et très - vieux; Mais il
And my suit - or is ver - y old, But he's

par - le de ma - ri - a - ge!
rich and of - fers me marriage.

Frasquita. (haughtily.)

Je me
Then he

cam-pe sur son che-val, Et dans la montagne il m'en-traî-ne!
lifts me up on his horse And speeds me a-way to the moun-tains!

Mercedes.
f
Dans
We

un château presque ro-yal, Le mien m'installe en souve-rai-ne!
live in a pal-ace of course, With gar-dens and statues and fountains,

Frasquita *p poco ritenuto.*

De l'a-mour à n'en plus fi-nir, Tous les
And his ar-dor nev-er grows cold. Ev-'ry

poco ritenuto.

a tempo.
Mercedes.
cresc.

jours, nou-vel-les fo-li-es! De l'or tant que j'en puis te-nir, Des di-a-
day un-end-ing em-braces. I've bar-rels and bar-rels of gold, Di-amonds,

a tempo
pp

270

18117

moi d'abord,   Ensui-te lui   pour tous les deux,   la mort!
First for me,   then for him.   But all the same,   it's death!

by retaining D♮ instead of taking D♭, one may transpose a semitone higher (F♯ minor instead of F minor) to the sign ⊕ on p. **274**; then execute the **2** measures A and B in small notes, as written, and proceed to the next.

En vain pour é - vi - ter les ré - ponses a -
You can't e - vade the truth the cards are say-ing

mères,   En vain tu   mê - le - ras,   Ce - la ne sert a -
clearly,   No mat - ter   how you try.   No use to deal a -

rien, les car - tes sont sin - cè - res   Et ne men - ti - ront pas!
gain, they're tell - ing you sin - cerely,   The cards will nev - er lie!

Dans le li-vre d'en haut si ta page est heu-reuse, Mêle et cou-pe sans peur:
If Fate saved you a happy page with-in its book, No need for anxiousness.

poco sf *pp*

La car-te sous tes doigts se tour-ne-ra joy-euse, T'annonçant
You know you'll get a luck-y card be-fore you look, Your fate is

le bon-heur! Mais si tu dois mou-rir, Si le mot re-dou-
happi-ness. But if your time has come and you are e-vil-

poco cresc.

table Est é-crit par le sort, Recom-mence vingt
starred, And if the end is near, You can try twen-ty

fois, la carte im-pi-to-yable Ré-pé-te-ra: la mort!
times, the un-re-lenting card Will re-ap-pear once more.

Di - tes-nous qui nous ai - me - ra!
And — which one will be true to us.

tes-nous qui nous tra - hi - ra!
lov - er will be treach-er - ous,

Di -
And —

En - cor!
Once more!

Par - lez en - cor! Par -
We want to know, we

tes-nous qui nous ai - me - ra! Par - lez en - cor! Par -
which one will be true to us. We want to know, we

Le dé - ses - poir!
My death is near!

lez en - cor! Di - tes-nous qui nous tra - hi - ra, Di -
want to know Which one we should be wa - ry of, Which

lez en - cor! Di - tes-nous qui nous tra - hi - ra, Di -
want to know Which one we should be wa - ry of, Which

La mort! la mort! En -
Once more, once more! My

Nº 20ᵇⁱˢ. Recitative.

pri - ses! J'ai sur la brèche où nous de-vons pas -
spot. ___ Close to the pass, three guards are on pa -

ser vu trois doua-niers! Il faut nous en dé-bar-ras-
trol. That might mean trouble. We must get them out of the

Carmen. *alla misura.*

ser. Pre - nez les bal-lots, et par -
way. This is an as-sign-ment for

tons; ___ Il faut pas - ser ___ nous pas-se - rons!
us. ___ We must get through, ___ and so we shall! ___

№ 21. Ensemble with Chorus.

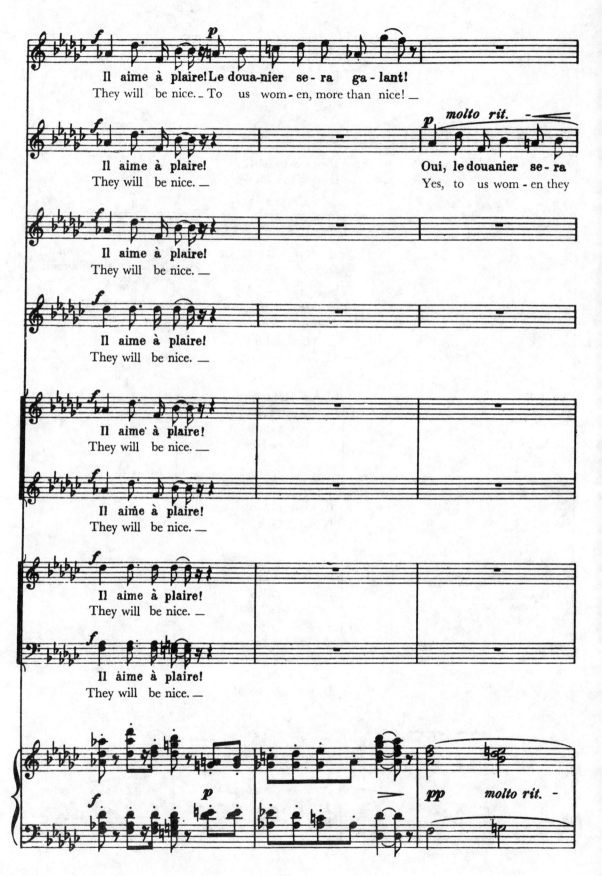

290

12117

El Remendado and El Dancaïro.

TENORS.

BASSES.

fai - re le ga - lant! Ah!_____ Lais - sez - nous pas - ser en a -
anx - ious to be nice. So _____ we will suc - ceed at an - y

fai - re le ga - lant! Ah!_____ Lais - sez - nous pas - ser en a -
anx - ious to be nice. So _____ we will suc - ceed at an - y

fai - re le ga - lant! Ah!_____ Lais - sez - nous pas - ser en a -
anx - ious to be nice. So _____ we will suc - ceed at an - y

le ga - lant! Oui, pas - sez
to be nice. Clear the way,

fai - re le ga - lant!
anx - ious to be nice.

fai - re le ga - lant!
anx - ious to be nice.

le ga - lant! Oui, pas - sez
to be nice. Clear the way,

le ga - lant! Oui, pas -
to be nice. Clear the

296

12117

(Exeunt omnes.)

№ 22. Air

Moderato.

Micaela.

Piano.

p dolce.

Recit. **Micaela.**

C'est des contreban - diers le re - fuge or-di -
Here's where the smugglers hide With their con - tra-band

nai - re. Il est i - ci, je le ver - rai ___ Et le de -
boo - ty; So it is here I'll find Jo - sé, ___ And for his

voir que m'impo-sa sa mè - - re Sans trembler je l'accom-pli -
moth - er's sake I'll do my du - ty, For her sake conquer ev - 'ry

cœur_____ je___ meurs d'ef - froi!_____
heart_____ I___ know I was wrong!_____

un poco meno p

Seu - - le en ce lieu_ sau - va - - ge, Tou - te seu - le j'ai
Here_____ in this dread sur - round - - ing I'm a - lone and a -

cresc. molto

peur, mais j'ai tort d'a - voir peur;_____
fraid, But I will not de - spair!_____

cresc.

dim. p poco rit.

Vous me don - ne - rez du__ cou - ra - ge, Vous me_ pro - tè - ge - rez,_ Sei -
God in His kindness all__ a - bound - ing Will make me strong and hear __ my

sf *dim.* *p* *pp* *colla voce.*

a tempo. *mf*

gneur!_____ Je vais
prayer._____ I'll be

a tempo. *dim.*

Nọ 22ᵇⁱˢ. Recitative.

№ 23. Duo.

318

12117

El - le s'ap - pel - le?
What is her name?

ment. C'est u - ne Zinga - ra, mon cher.
are. A most ex - cit - ing gyp - sy girl.

Car -

(aside.)

Carmen!
Carmen?

men.
Carmen.

Car - men! oui, mon cher.
It is. That's her name.

Un poco meno mosso. (♩ = 96.)

colla voce.

Escamillo.

Elle avait pour a - mant, elle avait pour a - mant Un sol - dat qui ja -
The way the ru - mor goes She loved an - oth - er man, A sol - dier who de -

Don José.

pp (aside.)

Carmen!
Carmen!

dis a dé - ser - té pour el - le. Ils s'a - do - raient! mais c'est fi - ni, je
sert - ed his bri - gade to please her. A mad af - fair, but that of course was

Vous l'aimez, cepen -
You don't mind that at

crois, Les a - mours de Car - men ne durent pas six mois.
once, For the loves of a Carmen do not last six months.

dant!
all?

cresc.

Vous l'aimez, cepen - dant!
You don't mind that at all?

cresc.

Je l'ai - me!
I love her,

cresc.

Je l'ai — me, oui, mon
I love — her, yes I

cher, je l'ai - me, je l'aime à la fo - li - e! —
do. I love — her, my friend, I love her mad - ly. —

rall.   dim.   p   f

Tempo I. (♩=112.) **Don José.**

Mais pour nous enle -
But when an - y-one

ver nos fil - les de Bo - hê - me,
takes a gyp - sy from her peo - ple,

Sa - vez-vous bien — qu'il faut pa -
You know, of course, — he has to

fin__ ma co-lè-re Trouve à qui__ par-ler, Le sang,
stroke__ of good for-tune Brought my ri-val __ here? His blood

le__ ma-la-dres-se J'en ri-rais, vrai-ment! Cher-
stroke__ of good luck to find my ri-val __ here? I

oui, le sang, je l'es-pè-re, Va bien-tôt cou-ler!
will flow be-fore his sweet-heart, This will cost him dear.

cher__ la maî-tres-se Et trou-ver, trouver l'a-mant!
look__ for my sweet-heart And find her ca-va-lier.

Met-tez-vous en gar-de Et veil-lez__ sur vous!__
Man to man, I dare__ you, de-fend__ your life.__

Met-tez-vous en gar-de Et veil-lez__ sur vous!__
Man to man, I dare__ you, de-fend__ your life.__

Met-tez-vous en gar-de Et veil-lez__ sur vous! Tant
Man to man, I dare__ you, de-fend__ your life. We'll

Met-tez-vous en gar-de Et veil-lez__ sur vous!
Man to man, I dare__ you, de-fend__ your life.

L'istesso tempo.

veil - lez _____ sur vous! _____
De - fend _____ your life! _____

(They fight.)

veil - lez _____ sur vous! _____
De - fend _____ your life! _____

L'istesso tempo.

tutta forza.

(Escamillo's knife snaps. Don José is about to strike him.)

fff

Ped.

attacca.

Nº 24. Finale.

men, qui me sauviez la vi - - e!___ Quant à
man to owe my life to Car - - men.___ As for

toi,___ beau sol-dat, Nous sommes manche à man - che, et
you,___ sol-dier-friend, The fight is un - de - cid - ed, But

nous jouer-ons la bel - le, oui, nous jouerons la bel - -
we'll re - new the du - el, Yes, we'll re - new the du - -

le, Le jour où tu vou-dras re - pren - dre le com-
el. What-ev - er day you choose, I'll be___ at your com-

dit! _____ et je n'ai_ plus i - ci qu'à
tell. _____ So till_ we _ meet a - gain, I

fai - re mes a - dieux!__ (Exit Escamillo slowly; Don
bid you all fare - well. ___

José tries to attack him, but is held back by El Dancaïro and El Remendado.)

Allegro. (♩=120.)

Don José (to Carmen, menacingly, but restrainedly.)

Prends garde à toi— Car - men, je suis las de souf-
This is e - nough, you hear! Do not drive me too

322

12117

stringendo.

sé, tu me sui-vras, tu me sui-vras!
sé, Come home with me, Come home with me. (to Don José.)

Carmen.

Va - t'en, va - t'en, tu fe - ras
Go on, go on, it's bet - ter

bien, No - tre mé - tier ne te vaut rien.
thus, You nev - er did be - long to us.

Don José. (to Carmen.)

Tu me dis de la
So you want me to

Oui, tu devrais partir!
Yes, you had bet - ter go.

sui - vre!
leave you?

poco animando.

Tu me dis de la sui - vre!
So you want me to leave you!

Pour que
So that

toi, tu puis - se cou - rir
you can quick - ly run off

A - près ton nou - vel a -
In - to Es - ca - mil - lo's

cresc. molto

330

To - ré - a - dor,___ l'a - mour t'at - tend!___
To - re - a - dor, ___ Your prize is love! ___

(Curtain.)

End of Act III.

Entr'acte.

Allegro vivo. (♩.=80.)

Piano.

attacca.

Act IV.

A square in Sevilla. At back, the walls of the ancient amphitheatre; the entrance to the latter is closed by a long awning.

No 25. Chorus.*)

Allegro deciso.

Zuniga.

Sopranos. *Fan-girls.*

Tenors. *Orange-girls.*
Program-peddlers.

Basses. *Water-peddlers.*
Cigarette-peddlers.

Wine-peddlers.

Allegro deciso. (♩= 168.)

Piano.

(Curtain rises.)

*) Les théâtres qui voudraient intercaler un ballet au 4ᵉ Acte feront chanter ce Chœur avec le texte en italique en supprimant la partie de Zuniga. Si l'on exécute ce morceau sans la danse, il ne faut pas faire la reprise indiquée à la page 345.

*) In case it is desired to introduce a ballet in Act IV, the Chorus is then to sing the text marked with †, omitting the part of Zuniga. If this number is executed without ballet, the reprise indicated on p. 345 becomes superfluous.

A deux cuar-tos!
Dansez, dan-sez,
Buy a pro-gram,
Take your plac-es

A Gypsy (to Zuniga, who repulses him.)

Vou-lez - vous aus - si des lor-gnet - tes?
Au cor - té - ge des____ to - ré - ros.
Will you buy a fine pair of glass - es?
To ad - mire the great____ To - re - ros.

f. p.   *cresc.*   *f.*

I. & II.

A deux cuartos! | A deux cuartos! | A deux cuartos! | Voy - ez! à | deux cuar-tos!
Dansez, dan-sez, | *Dansez, dan-sez,* | *Dansez, dan-sez,* | *Dan-sez jeu - nes gar-çons,*
Just a quar-ter! | Buy a trin-ket! | Wine and wa-ter! | La - dies and | gen - tle - men!
for the danc-ing! | Take your plac-es | for the danc-ing! | La - dies and | gen - tle - men,

I. & II.

A deux cuartos! | A deux cuartos! | Voy - ez! à | deux cuar-tos!
Dansez, dan-sez, | *Dansez, dan-sez,* | *Dan-sez jeu - nes gar-çons,*
Buy a trin-ket! | Wine and wa-ter! | La - dies and | gen - tle - men!
Take your plac-es | for the danc-ing! | La - dies and | gen - tle - men,

I. & II.

Se - ño - ras et Ca - bal - le - - - - -
Oui, dan - sez jeu - nes__ fil - let - - - - -
Se - ño - ras and Ca - bal - le - - - - -
Se - ño - ras and Ca - bal - le - - - - -

1.

Se - ño - ras et Ca - bal - le - - - - -
Oui, dan - sez jeu - nes__ fil - let -
Se - ño - ras and Ca - bal - le - - - - -
Se - ño - ras and Ca - bal - le - - - - -

1.

№ 26. March and Chorus.

*) A cuadrilla, at a Spanish festival, is a group of performers distinguished from the rest by colors, insignia, or uniforms.

La qua - dril - le des To - ré - ros! Les voi - ci!
We sa - lute the brave To - re - ros, Here they come!

La qua - dril - le des To - ré - ros! Les voi - ci!
We sa - lute the brave To - re - ros, Here they come!

La qua - dril - le des To - ré - ros! Les voi - ci! les voi - ci!
We sa - lute the brave To - re - ros, Here they come, here they come!

Les voi - ci! les voi - ci! les voi - ci!
Here they come, here they come here they come!

(The procession begins. — The words of the chorus indicate the stage-arrangement.)

CHILDREN.

ben ritmato.

Voi-ci, dé - bou-chant sur la pla - ce, Voi-ci d'a - bord, marchant au pas,—
Now it's time for boo-ing and hiss-ing. There's the sher-iff, mean as can be,—

Voi-ci d'a-bord, marchant au pas, L'al - gua-zil à vi - lai - ne _ fa - ce.
No one is as nas-ty as he. On hol - i-days he's nev-er_miss-ing!

À bas! à bas! à bas! à bas!
A-way, go home, a-way, go home!

SOPRANOS.

TENORS.

À bas l'Al-gua-zil! à bas!
We don't want you here, go home!

BASSES.

TENORS.

Et puis sa - lu - ons au pas -
See them march a - long, proud and

BASSES.

sa - - ge, Sa - lu - ons les har - dis Chu -
har - - dy. Give a cheer for the Chu - los,

los! _____ Bra - vo! vi - va!
too. _____ Bra - vo! Bra - vo!

Ban - de - ril - le - ros!
Ban - de - ril - la - men!

Ban - de - ril - le - ros!
Ban - de - ril - la - men!

Ban - de - ril - le - ros!
Ban - de - ril - la - men!

CHILDREN.

Une au - tre qua - dril - le s'a - vance!
An - oth - er quad - rille is ap - proaching!

SOPRANOS.

Une au - tre qua - dril - le s'a -
An - oth - er quad - rille is ap -

(Escamillo enters; beside him Carmen, radiant with delight, and brilliantly dressed.)

Vive Es-ca-mil-lo! Vive Es-ca-mil-lo! Ah!
Hail Es-ca-mil-lo! Hail Es-ca-mil-lo! Ah!

Vive Es-ca-mil-lo! Vive Es-ca-mil-lo! Ah!
Hail Es-ca-mil-lo! Hail Es-ca-mil-lo! Ah!

Vive Es-ca-mil-lo! Vive Es-ca-mil-lo! Ah!
Hail Es-ca-mil-lo! Hail Es-ca-mil-lo! Ah!

bra - vo! Les voi-ci! voi - ci la qua-dril-le, La qua-dril - le
bra - vo! Look at him, so hand-some and dash-ing, We sa-lute the

bra - vo! Les voi-ci! voi - ci la qua-dril-le, La qua-dril - le
bra - vo! Look at him, so hand-some and dash-ing, We sa-lute the

bra - vo! Les voi-ci! voi - ci la qua-dril-le, La qua-dril - le
bra - vo! Look at him, so hand-some and dash-ing, We sa-lute the

12117

(breve)

moi! Si tu m'ai -- mes, __ si tu m'ai -
me, __ If you love _____ me, __ if you love

Carmen. *p espress.*

Ah! je t'aime, Es - ca - mil - lo, je t'aime et que je
I am yours, Es - ca - mil - lo, And may God be my

mes! __
me. __

meu - re, Si __ j'ai ja - mais ai - mé quel - qu'un au - tant que
wit - ness, I __ nev - er loved a man with such pas - sion be -

toi! __ Ah! je t'ai -- me __ Oui, je t'ai -
fore! How I love _____ you, __ How I love __

Escamillo.

Ah! je t'ai -- me Oui, je t'ai -
How I love _____ you, __ How I love __

tends, et je vais lui par - ler.___
stay, and I'll wait for him here.___

Mercedes.

Car-
I

Carmen.

men,___ crois - moi,___ prends gar - de! Je ne crains
beg you, be - lieve me, don't stay here. I'm not a-

Frasquita.

rien!___ Prends gar - de!
fraid.___ Be care - ful!

a po - co a po -

co cre - scen - do ed ac - ce - le - ran - do fi - no al

Tempo I. Allegro. (♩ = 116.)

(The crowd has entered the amphitheatre; Frasquita and Mercedes also go in. Carmen and

Don José are left alone.)

attacca.

№ 27. Duet and final Chorus.

Don José.

Mais je suis brave _ et n'ai pas vou-lu fuir. Je ne me - na - ce
But I have cour-age and de - cid - ed to stay. I do not mean you

pas _ j'im - plo - re, je sup - pli - e! No - tre pas - sé, _ Car-
harm, I beg you, I im - plore you. What used to be _ is

men, no - tre pas-sé, je l'ou - bli - e! Oui, _ nous al - lons tous
done, _ The past is dead, _ it is o - ver. Yes, _ we'll start life a-

deux _ Com-men - cer _ une au - tre vi - e, Loin d'i-
new. _ It will be _ a new ex - ist - ence, Far a-

Carmen.

Tu deman-des l'im-pos - si - ble! Carmen jamais n'a men-
You are talk-ing like a dream-er. I won't lie, I won't pre-

ci _ sous d'autres cieux!
way, _ for me and you.

ti; Son â - me reste in - fle - xi - ble; Entre elle et
tend! What was be - tween us is o - ver. Once and for

toi___ tout est fi - ni. Ja - mais je n'ai men - ti;___ En - tre
all,___ this is the end! You know, I nev - er lie,___ Once for

nous, tout est fi - ni. Car - men,___ il est temps en -
all, this is good - bye. Car - men, oh let me per -

co - re, Oui,___ il est temps en - co - re___ Ô
suade you, Yes,___ life is still be - fore you. I

ma Carmen, laisse-moi Te sau-ver, toi que j'a - do - re. Ah!
beg of you, please, come a - way with me, For I a - dore you. Ah,

12117
Music from the sign ⊕ to ⊕ on p. 377 may be skipped.

376

12117

Non, ce cœur n'est plus à toi,
No, my love for you is dead.

lais-se-moi te sau-ver Et me sau-ver a-vec
Car-men, come a-way with me, We both can be hap-py

En vain tu dis: "Je t'a-dore!" Tu n'ob-tien-dras
I will not hear what you say. There's no hope

toi, Ô ma Car-men, il est temps en-co-re, Ah! laisse-
still. Oh, come with me, life is still be-fore you. Ah, come a-

rien, non, rien de moi, Ah! c'est en vain.
you. My love is dead, you hope in vain.

moi Te sau-ver, Carmen,
way, come with me a-gain.

Ah! laisse-moi te sau-
Ah! Car-men, let me per-

tu vou-dras— Tout! tu m'en-tends,____ tout, tu m'en-
an - y - thing, Yes, all you ask, ____ Yes, all you

tends,____ tout!____ Mais ne me quit-te pas, Ô
ask,____ all,____ If on - ly you will come with

ma Car - men, Ah! sou-viens-toi, sou-viens-toi
me a - gain! Those gol - den days, have you for -

du pas - sé! Nous nous aimions, na - guè - re!
got - ten them?____ How much we loved each oth - er!

(with desperation)
Ah! ne me quit - te pas, Car - men, ah! ne me quit - te
O Car - men, do not leave me now! O, do not leave me

Carmen.

pas! Ja-mais Car - men___ ne cè-de - ra!___
now! I won't give in, ___ this is good-bye! ___

Li - bre elle est née et li - bre el-le mour - -
Free I was born, and free I ___ shall

(Hearing the cries of the crowd in the amphitheatre, applauding Escamillo, Carmen makes a gesture of delight. — Don José keeps his eyes fixed on her. — At the end of the chorus, Carmen attempts to enter the amphitheatre; but Don José steps in front of her.)

Allegro giocoso.

ra!
die!

SOPRANOS.

Vi - va! vi - va! la course est bel - le! Vi - va! sur le sa - ble san-glant,
Now the fight is get - ting ex - cit - ing. See the bull is rag - ing mad - ly.

TENORS.

Vi - va! vi - va! la course est bel - le! Vi - va! sur le sa - ble san-glant,
Now the fight is get - ting ex - cit - ing. See the bull is rag - ing mad - ly,

BASSES.

Allegro giocoso. ($\flat$ = 116.)

ff (Fanfare behind the scenes.)

Le taureau, le taureau s'é-lan-ce! Voy-ez, voy-ez, voy-ez, voy-
Run-ning wild-ly, he charg-es for-ward. Hur-rah, hur-rah, hur-rah! Hur-

Le taureau, le taureau s'é-lan-ce! Voy-ez, voy-ez, voy-
Run-ning wild-ly, he charg-es for-ward. Hur-rah, hur-rah! Hur-

Voy-
Hur-

ez!— Le tau-reau qu'on harcèle En bon-dis-sant s'é-lan-ce, Voy-ez!
rah! It's a mar-ve-lous fight. With light-ning speed he charg-es a-gain!

ez! Le tau-reau qu'on harcèle En bon-dis-sant s'é-lan-ce, Voy-ez!
rah! It's a mar-ve-lous fight. With light-ning speed he charg-es a-gain!

Frap-pé jus-te, juste en plein cœur! Voy-ez!
Es-ca-mil-lo, now show your skill. Hur-rah!

Frap-pé jus-te, juste en plein cœur! Voy-ez, voy-ez!
Es-ca-mil-lo, now show your skill. Hur-rah, hur-rah!

Voy-ez, voy-ez, voy-ez!
Hur-rah, hur-rah, hur-rah!

Allegro giocoso. (Carmen again tries to enter the amphitheatre, Don José stops her again.)

me!
him!

SOPRANOS.

Vi - va! vi - va! la course est bel - le! Vi - va! sur le
Bra - vo, bra - vo! This is ex - cit - ing. Now the bull is

TENORS.

Vi - va! vi - va! la course est bel - le! Vi - va! sur le
Bra - vo, bra - vo! This is ex - cit - ing. Now the bull is

BASSES.

Vi - va! vi - va! la course est bel - le! Vi - va! sur le
Bra - vo, bra - vo! This is ex - cit - ing. Now the bull is

Allegro giocoso. (♩ = 116)

(Fanfare behind the scenes.)

sa - ble san - glant, Le tau - reau, le tau - reau s'é - lan - ce!
rag - ing mad - ly, Run - ning wild - ly, pierced by the lanc - es!

sa - ble san - glant, Le tau - reau, le tau - reau s'é - lan - ce!
rag - ing mad - ly, Run - ning wild - ly, pierced by the lanc - es!

sa - ble san - glant, Le tau - reau, le tau - reau s'é - lan - ce!
rag - ing mad - ly, Run - ning wild - ly, pierced by the lanc - es!

(Carmen attempts to escape, but Don José catches up with her at the entrance of the amphitheatre; he stabs her; she falls, and dies.)

(The crowd reënters the stage.)   Andante moderato.

To - ré - a - dor, _____ l'a - mour t'at - tend!
To - re - a - dor, _____ your prize is love!

Andante moderato. (♩=76)

ff

Don José.

Vous pou-vez m'ar-rê - ter. _____ C'est moi qui l'ai tu-
I have killed my own love! _____ I killed the one I

fp   ff   fp

é - e! Ah! Car - men! _____ ma Car - men _____ a - do-
love! _____ She is dead! _____ O my Car - men, _____ how I

f   cresc.   ff

cresc. - - -f

(Curtain.)

ré - e!
loved you!

f   p   f   p   ff